MW01489513

BLANK TO BANK:
HOW TO STRATEGICALLY SPOT TRENDS AND UNIQUELY LEVERAGE THEM TO
BUILD A PRINT ON DEMAND EMPIRE

CONTENTS

CONTENTS

Brittany Lewis

Hi! My name is Brittany and I am absolutely in love with teaching people how to create total financial and lifestyle freedom for themselves by leveraging print on demand as a business model and Etsy as a platform.

PRINT ON DEMAND AND ETSY IS A MATCH MADE IN HEAVEN.

So many of my students have soared passed the 6-figure mark in their shops by utilizing this dynamic business duo.

I did it myself as well, and honestly? **My life has been pretty much pure magic ever since.**

For the most part, I teach how to sell t-shirts, sweatshirts, and hoodies because I believe they have the best profit margins and the most opportunity (when you know where to look!).

But you can apply what you learn in this book to any variety of P.O.D. products.

All that being said, I've spent almost 10 years now studying the print on demand business and figuring out how to make it work for me. I didn't just want "OK". I wanted a shop that was ON FIRE.

Along this journey, I discovered a few simple tricks that helped me realize that, with the right strategy, **print on demand does really work** and it can work really well for anyone if they know the right stuff.

For the last few years I've worked with thousands of online sellers teaching them my strategy and how to take meaningful steps to create a successful print on demand online presence.

I began in 2014 with no experience and no expectations. I was buying old jeans from Goodwill and cutting them into high waisted shorts for myself. I figured it might be fun to sell them!

Low and behold, it worked! And pretty fast... I was a 6-figure Etsy seller within about 18 months of opening.

I discovered print on demand years after I was creating products by hand (and I hated the production side of it). **Print on demand opened up a whole new world of possibility.**

This is me wearing the first pair of shorts I created for my shop in 2014. I hand painted a galaxy print on the front (they soon after became my top seller!).

Immediately I recognized there was no ceiling to it - the sky was the limit! It was so exciting to realize that *now I had a business model that would allow me to focus on being creative* - and the rest was taken care of by my partner manufacturer!

Back then, there were no Etsy gurus, ebooks, or even many YouTube videos about how to sell on Etsy... So I spent years trial and erroring my way through and ended up creating my own unique system of highly specific (and *very* effective) strategies.

I became the research and data-based decision making QUEEN.

This is <u>*the very first time*</u> I'm releasing this information all in one place and I cannot wait to do so!

Before we begin...

I'm passionate about sharing this knowledge and writing this book because I know firsthand how much potential print on demand holds.

However, many sellers jump in feet first and quickly discover that, without a strategy, it's easy to get buried under the competition. Every business comes with its challenges and print on demand is no exception.

When the pressure is on, sellers will either abandon their online shops entirely or look for a new business model entirely because they can't seem to crack the code and figure out how to make things work.

I'm here to tell you, *it doesn't have to be this way.*

When I first began, I had zero experience selling online and I had even less experience with graphic design - which are two things one might assume are necessities if you're to reach any level of success in a print on demand business.

But it's just simply not the case.

I've sold over $95k+ of my products this year (6 months in) and am set to make just as much, if not more, in the remainder of the year...

This year: Jan - Jul 2020 ▾   ⟳ Just now

Visits	Orders	Conversion rate	Revenue
144.2K	3,292	2.3%	$92,523.98

This has been possible mainly because of the things I'm going to share with you in this book.

I've learned how to spot trends that are in demand and create designs that people are actually actively searching for on Etsy (and really want to buy).

More importantly, I've learned equally as simple ways *to create these types of results over and over again.*

The reason I decided to write this book was to share what's worked for me, which is **a specific strategy I've developed in order to create big results in my business *without* needing e-commerce or graphic design experience.**

<u>Anyone can do this.</u> I know because I've taught many sellers who had little to no faith in their e-commerce potential, but together we turned that *all* the way around!

My goal here is to help guide you through the main stumbling blocks I've seen get in the way of the majority of my clients when trying to get the ball rolling.

What is the main stumbling block? First, how to find the hottest items on the market and second, how to create designs for that same type of demand that potential customers will actually care about enough to want to purchase.

I understand this issue **in and out** because I dealt with it myself. It was tricky BUT… I knew the print on demand opportunity was too large to just scrap altogether.

I had to find out how to make it work. *And I did.*

Blank to Bank is not a sales pitch. I assure you it is jam packed with **real value** that you can utilize and implement in your business right away.

However, if you would like to dive deeper into my world, I have tons of resources to help your business soar. Here's a few before we get started:

Instagram:
www.instagram.com/beawolfbiz

Free Mastermind Facebook Group:
www.facebook.com/groups/beawolfbiz

And if print on demand is something you're 100% all in with and ready to learn *all my unique strategies* to build to 6-figures on Etsy from A-Z, then you simply **must watch** my completely free masterclass:
"Top 3 Strategies of $100k+ Mega Sellers On Etsy":
www.beawolfbiz.com/starthere

Watching this masterclass will be one of the single best things you do (aside from reading this book) to accelerate your print on demand journey to success!

Introduction

HOW MY BUSINESS WENT
FROM BLANK TO BANK

When I first stumbled upon print on demand it was like discovering a business opportunity utopia.

It caught my attention *immediately*.

By that time, I had been selling on Etsy for a few years and was simply exhausted. I was screen printing and sponge painting my life away every single day, creating and shipping all of my products by hand.

I was selling tons of items and was constantly slammed with production tasks.

I was busy doing things I didn't necessarily love to do.

I wanted to work ON my business, not IN my business doing production and wearing all the hats myself, which is a common plight of many business owners, am I right?

Print on demand allows sellers to focus on what they want. It takes all the production and shipping hassle off of sellers shoulders and gets their orders fulfilled from start to finish for them.

A dream come true, perhaps?

I certainly think so!

And so do many of the clients I've worked with to develop their print on demand shops over the years.

The sky is the limit as to what kind of online store you can create with a great print on demand partner on your side.

There *is* a bit of inherent trickiness here, however.

You see, due to the level of ease that this business model allows for online sellers, there are many shops trying to get a piece of the action for themselves.

It's a competitive space, as so many e-commerce businesses are.

But fear not! I've spent *almost 10 years and countless hours* figuring out the exact formula to rise to the top despite any market saturation.

My online shops have accumulated well over $600k+ in revenue and the process I use to create these types of results has continued to work for me and my clients in a predictable, consistent way.

It's the same process I'm sharing with you in this book.

So listen, I hope you're ready to get your mind blown and to start making some serious cash online!

In this book

I'M GOING TO REVEAL...

• The <u>exact process</u> I've perfected over the years for finding the hottest current trends to make your print on demand shop explode, *even if you have zero previous experience selling online.*

• Why print on demand is **the business model with the most potential to make you bank** in the shortest amount of time and without many of the usual e-commerce headaches.

• *Exactly* how to let current trends <u>do the work for you</u> with your designs and how to determine the specific market for your shop that **will garner tons of attention and sales.**

• **The number one reason most people end up failing in their print on demand business.**

• ALL (and *I mean all*) the trend-spotting and design creation resources I've collected over the years that have helped me create a shop that's in the top 1% of sellers on Etsy and **rakes in constant sales for me every single day** (with very little upkeep)!

• ...And so much more!

01 Wait...
WHAT IN THE WORLD IS PRINT ON DEMAND?

If you're already familiar with print on demand, go ahead and skip to the next chapter, but newbies... listen up!

Print on demand companies are considered "partner manufacturers" to brands who want to create a hands-off process in fulfilling orders for their customers.

Direct-to-garment (DTG) printing and embroidery are the two most common services these P.O.D. companies offer.

Here's how the process works...

Basically, you sign up with a print on demand company of your choice (I love & recommend Printify.com or Printful.com), which is typically free.

You can then integrate your shop with that supplier with a stand alone website (like Shopify) or a shop you own within a larger marketplace (like Etsy, as I recommend).

Most print on demand companies offer a wide variety of platforms they integrate with, so no matter where you are selling, chances are you can seamlessly integrate print on demand items there (and the integration literally takes seconds!).

Once you've integrated your shop and set up some simple payment options (credit/debit card and/or PayPal account), you can then browse the product offering (catalog) that print on demand company provides.

You then choose the items you'd like to offer in your shop and can begin placing your designs wherever you want them onto a digital mockup right away!

If your brain is having a bit of trouble wrapping itself around this process, on the next page I've got a visual for how it works...

YOUR DESIGN + **DIGITAL MOCKUP** = **NEW LISTING**

After you complete this process, you then publish these items to your shop, which happens with a click of a button, and voilà!

Your first product is set up and ready to purchase within your shop.

It truly is that simple and can take about 10-20 minutes to go from no shop to a shop with your first published item using print on demand!

After you get a few products in your shop and sales start rolling in, those sales are pushed directly to the P.O.D. company and fulfillment starts automatically.

There is nothing else you have to do! The item will be printed, packed and shipped directly to your customer after the order is placed.

One of the many beauties of print on demand is that you are only charged as each order is placed.

If a customer places an order for a t-shirt and pays, let's say $22 dollars for it with $4 dollar shipping, that order is then pushed to your P.O.D. provider, who will charge you (once the order processes) for the cost of the item and the shipping (shirts can range anywhere from $5-$15 and shipping is typically around $4-$8).

This is what makes print on demand a great option for new business owners who are starting with very little capital.

Or for someone who just doesn't want to invest a ton of money into inventory that may not sell like crazy at first while they're still learning.

No wasted cash!

Talk about a dream business model, right?

You can start a brand in minutes with very little initial monetary investment – if any at all.

Another advantage of P.O.D. is that you can create and list a product in a matter of minutes. The ability to go from a single idea to a complete, sellable manifestation within the timeframe of basically a commercial break is a pretty darn useful upside, don't you think?

I've spotted a great design idea at the mall and on the drive home, in my head, adapted a unique version of a similar concept that fit my target market more specifically.

I hopped on my laptop as soon as I got home and was making sales on that product by the next day.

This type of scenario has happened many times, and I must be honest, it creates quite a visceral satisfaction every time.

That kind of fast paced progress is addicting when you're someone who loves to see results.

The best part? Anyone can do this!

It just takes a bit of know-how... So *let's talk about that know-how!*

02 A common
PRINT ON DEMAND MISSTEP...

We've covered how print on demand is a great business model because it allows you to act quickly and efficiently once you've brewed up a new idea based on your research.

The sooner you can take advantage of high demand with unique designs, the faster you can start raking in the big bucks selling your items!

Print on demand gives sellers a quickness and efficiency your typical online retail business model can't offer.

But you may now be saying, "Alright. I'm convinced it's a good business model but, Brittany, you don't understand! I've got no idea where to start when it comes to 'trend'!"

Heck, you might even be someone who couldn't name a single designer brand if you absolutely had to.

Even so, *relax*… you're in good hands here! No prior trendy track record required.

I want to share with you exactly how I spot trends and **one secret trick that will help you leverage those trends in a special way that will skyrocket you ahead of your competition (really!).**

The goal is to have the speed and efficiency of print on demand on your side, plus a sharp strategy for producing winning designs.

That's a serious combo right there!

The most important part is, however, that it does work.

I am a walking testament to the viability of print on demand as a serious, full time business and I am hell bent on showing other sellers how to get there as well!

Before we get into the exact strategy, I want to speak quickly as to why you shouldn't do what's easy – meaning what just about everyone else is doing.

For instance, say Fourth of July is around the corner... You should probably create a print on demand tee featuring an American flag, right?

Maybe one that says "Happy Fourth" in red, white, and blue and some colorful fireworks?

Just no. Please...please no.

It's not that these designs aren't lovely...

Or even that nobody wants them...

It's that almost every other shop is already selling them.

This type of generic design creation is the number one reason most print on demand sellers fail.

Now, I get it – it seems a little confusing, because on one hand, I'm telling you that you must capitalize on trends and learn how to spot them.

But on the other, I'm telling you that you should never sell the usual holiday designs that so many other sellers are cashing in with.

Well, the truth is... You can certainly sell holiday themed designs, but recreating the typical designs you see in thousands of other shops *is a losing strategy.*

Because, HELLO?? Tens, or even hundreds, of thousands of sellers are already doing that.

So sure, you might make a few sales with this approach if you're lucky...

But we want you drowning in sales.

How do you get to that point with your print on demand shop?

Keep reading... *Trust me*, the following chapters unveil everything you need to know...

03
PART 1

Why, oh why
DO WE RESEARCH??

So, as a print on demand mentor I kind of have a "thing"...

Everyone who follows me knows I am relentless and *downright ruthless* about this one foundational thing that makes all the difference in building a successful print on demand shop.

That thing is **research.**

That's why I've taken the time to dedicate an entire ebook to it. Because, in my experience, it's the vital missing piece in so many sellers' print on demand puzzles.

Now, there are a lot of misconceptions around the word research so before you write me off because researching sounds boring - give me a chance here!

Research means the same thing to me as trend-spotting, or what I like to call, brain priming.

It's not about spreadsheets, rigid note taking, numbers or mind boggling amounts of information.

It's about having fun observing current demand wherever you can on the internet (or in real life!).

I call it brain priming because researching is literally the act of priming your brain to understand demand.

Because when you understand demand, you can create designs that are in demand – and creating designs that are in demand is how you go from BLANK TO BANK.

Are you following?

You can't make sales from stuff people don't want or aren't actively searching for. And you can't create stuff people DO want unless you have a solid understanding of what that currently looks like at any given time.

So you must prime your brain to know what's currently in demand, so you can create best selling designs with ease!

When you look at it this way... Isn't research starting to look kinda *sexy*?

If so, GOOD.

It is!

It's your **sexy missing link** that most sellers never take the time to dial in on.

But not you... I know you're smarter than that.

03

PART 2

What in the hell IS A MENTAL ARCHIVE?

We now understand why it's so important to become an avid researcher and what exactly it means to "brain prime".

Now I want to talk about another special little phrase I coined called the *mental archive*.

It sounds weird - but stick with me again here. It's SUPER important...

What is it?

A mental archive is a place in your mind/subconscious where all the details and information you've gathered through research in regards to current demand & trends is stored.

To the right are a few examples of what print on demand designs usually look like when the seller hasn't done much research (and therefore has a small, or even non-existent, mental archive)...

These designs aren't great, and they're not likely to stand out or captivate a shopper enough to prompt a sale.

SMALL MENTAL ARCHIVE

The photos on the left are some examples of what print on demand designs usually look like when the seller DOES make research a priority and has spent time building their mental archive.

Note how the niche/theme in all these examples are the same, but the designs are *drastically* different...

LARGE MENTAL ARCHIVE

You see, when you understand the power of research and you commit to building your mental archive from the start... you eliminate months, even YEARS in some cases, of throwing stuff at the wall and having nothing stick.

I like to think of your mental archive like a bucket. The more you're researching (and we'll get into the specifics of this process in a bit), the fuller your bucket (or mental archive) becomes.

When you've got a full bucket, you've got plenty of juice to power some serious creativity and ideas that will ultimately land you a shop full of best sellers if you're doing all this the right way.

With a robust mental archive built from many hours of dedicated research, the design creation process becomes more and more effortless, because you begin to "just know" what to do.

But it's not magic! It's your well-primed subconscious doing the heavy lifting for you.

Research in different areas...

This is why, when you first begin, designing feels HIGH EFFORT and confusing. It takes forever and you get stuck often.

It's because your mental archive is still small.

BEGINNER MENTAL ARCHIVE   **ADVANCED SELLER MENTAL ARCHIVE**

The more quality research you do, the faster your mental archive grows.

Most sellers don't ever build a mental archive at all and so they try to build a 6-figure shop while missing basically the only absolutely essential thing you need in order to do so.

Without a mental archive to draw on, sellers continue to flail around, get discouraged and demotivated, and then quit in despair.

Trying to create mountains of sales in a print on demand shop without an ever-growing mental archive is like trying to grow a lush garden in a desert.

You're choosing an uphill battle by continuing to try to create best selling designs when you have little to no real knowledge to draw upon when it comes to what a best selling design is actually composed of.

I don't like uphill battles do you? I'm certainly not cool with deliberately choosing one for myself **when there's clearly a better way.**

04 The Strategy

PART 1

Hopefully by now I've convinced you of the true value of a solid research process when it comes to building a massive print on demand shop.

If you're not convinced, go back and read the last section again (it's important this really sinks in!) - then proceed with the following strategic outline...

Are you ready?

Ok, so it all starts with my favorite trifecta...

Fire up that laptop and open up tabs for Etsy.com, Pinterest.com and grab your phone to hop on Instagram.

Why these platforms? Well, the reason for Etsy should be obvious... What better place to research what Etsy shoppers want than on Etsy?

As for Pinterest, it has **463 million users *per month***. So there's an abundance of great up-to-date in demand content always circulating there.

And instagram? It's basically a print on demand researchers' dream. There are SO many different ways to leverage Instagram to build your mental archive. I'll touch on that in a bit.

Keep in mind these are my top three places to research, but they are by no means the only places you should be brain priming and getting ideas.

Be open to looking *everywhere and anywhere* (including trendy big brands like Pacsun.com or UrbanOutfitters.com or any other stores that might fit the niches you're looking into).

This process is NOT black and white and should not be rigid. It's meant to serve your creativity, so allow it to be free and flow-ey and, most importantly, **have fun with it!**

"Ok, Brittany... But how do I know where to start?"

This is really the easiest part that sellers make into the hardest part because _they overthink it._

Allow me to break it down for you...

Let's say I'm looking around on Etsy and I'm letting curiosity lead the way. There's no rush, no force, just me being curious about what people are shopping for lately.

I'm keeping an eye out for best seller badges, "20 people have this in their cart" notifications, or "Etsy's Pick" badges.

Why? Because *this tells me where the demand is*. If it has a best seller badge, or any of the other things listed above, I know that people are paying attention to that listing and want it. **That's a big green flag.**

Say I want to just start anywhere to start getting some general ideas of where to research. I type in "women's shirt" into the search bar because I know I can start general if I'm just getting a sense of where to begin.

In those search results, I come across this listing shown below. It interests me because I spot the best seller badge associated with it. I click on it to examine the listing further...

14 views in the last 24 hours
Sale ends in 32 minutes

$18.36+ ~~$22.95+~~ (20% Off)

Comfort Colors® Shirt, Flowers Shirt, Wildflower Shirt, Women Shirt, Botanical Shirt, Nature Lover Shirt, Spring Shirt, Flower Gardener Gift

Since this listing has a best seller badge, they're doing something right. Maybe *a lot of things right*! But one thing we know for sure is that their design has demand.

So it's worth paying attention to.

(*A special note about this:* we are <u>never</u> researching to copy other sellers. That is lazy, ineffective, and just downright icky. The point of paying attention to what's working is to learn what's working as a whole, not to blatantly rip off what already exists. We're getting inspired to create unique versions of what we understand has demand in a general sense.)

Back to the above example: Since this is a best seller design, we can examine all of the listing details, including the title, to get some ideas.

The beauty of this is that you can get some brilliant keyword ideas to begin your research right in the titles of these listings.

The point isn't to nail the perfect niche to research on your first try - it's simply to be led by curiosity. Like a kind of, "I wonder what this is all about" vibe.

Looking at the above listing's title, we may choose to look into "wildflower", "botanical" or "nature lover" products.

You might be curious enough that you go directly back into the Etsy search bar and type in "wildflower shirt"... And guess what?

You're researching, baby!

It gets to be this simple. *Don't overthink it.*

But you have to understand the answers won't be handed to you. You have to do some digging. You have to be willing to work a little. It takes what it takes!

And now you might be asking, but how do I know if what I'm researching has any demand?

Think back to what I said about best seller badges and other types of clues that alert us to demand.

Just look out for those clues in whatever niches you're looking into.

They're extremely useful in identifying what's hot!

ETSY

I've introduced you already to a bit of what the Etsy research phase looks like, but let's dive a little deeper.

Best seller badges and the like are important, and so is generally getting acquainted with the highest ranking listings (meaning all first page items, but you can ignore the built-in ads).

Why? These are the items that are getting the most attention from buyers – meaning they have the highest demand.

Listings don't get to the first page by accident. They're there because the algorithm has put them there, based on how many clicks/favorites/purchases (attention) that listing has been getting.

This isn't to say that the 2nd, 3rd, or 4th pages of search for any given phrase are useless - but the first page is where the heavy hitters are at in terms of attention, so spending time researching there is not a bad idea.

Because you're a seller looking to make it big on Etsy, this really is the best place to start - if we're speaking in terms of finding keywords to start researching and to begin your research in general!

Let's continue with our first example and say you found the "wildflower" keyword in that best selling listings' title and began to research it a bit on Etsy.

You then come across this listing in those search results and realize it's also a best seller:

In demand. 4 people bought this in the last 24 hours.
Sale ends in 2 hours
$11.94+ $19.90+ (40% Off)

Kindness Shirt, Inspirational Shirt, Kind Shirt, Be Kind Shirt, Flower Shirt, Spread Kindness Shirt, Motivational Shirt, Shirts For Women

You might notice some new keywords in this listing's title like "spread kindness" and "be kind shirt".

You could then choose to take a mental note of these keywords (or quickly jot them down for later reference) or go explore a bit of that potential trend as well immediately.

You shouldn't be constantly hopping from trend to trend and never absorbing anything during your research, but you should allow yourself to openly observe and go down what I like to call "rabbit holes" if something piques your curiosity.

I should also add, throughout this whole process, you want to be sure to be saving anything that interests you to a Pinterest board.

This just helps lessen overwhelm because you know you've got it saved and can go back and reference it in the future if needed.

QUICK TIP: Downloading the Pinterest widget to your desktop or on whatever device you're researching on is the easiest way to be able to "pin" images from anywhere quickly. To download this, simply give "Pinterest widget" a Google!

If all of this is seeming a little bit mind boggling at the moment, not to worry.

Diving in and putting it into practice will allow it to feel a lot less intimidating once you realize it's just a fun, easy process that you can spend as much or as little time on each day as you please (although I do recommend at least an hour a day!).

Let's move on to the 2nd puzzle piece in our research trifecta now...

PINTEREST

Above I outlined an example of how to begin your research process, but again, it's not a black and white regimen with any rules.

Using the Etsy > Pinterest > Instagram framework may be the easiest way to go about things for beginners, however.

If you're using Pinterest as your second step and you've found some ideas on Etsy, you can continue to flesh out those keywords with some additional brain priming on Pinterest.

Why isn't Etsy enough? Well, remember, the goal here is simply to build your mental archive as a whole. Be careful that you're not acting like a heat seeking missile and desperately trolling the internet for an idea that you can quickly turn into a design that'll catch fire by tomorrow morning.

Honestly, that's just not how things work. While researching, your focus shouldn't necessarily be, "What could I turn this into to get sales??". It should be much softer and more open. Your focus should be on simply observing for now.

Just let that mental archive grow (and the rest will flow, trust me).

OK, so let's say you continued your "wildflowers" search.

It's likely that if you search "wildflowers shirt" on Pinterest, the content will be mostly listings from Etsy.

Obviously, this isn't super useful since you've already researched this phrase on Etsy.

Do you bet I have a trick up my sleeve now?

You better believe it!

Searching for more t-shirt designs on Pinterest will not only just show us more of what we've seen on Etsy, but it's continuing to research what already exists on t-shirts.

Researching clothing directly has its merits, but it's not where you want to spend all your time while brain priming. Because there's even more opportunities to ignite your creativity and grow your mental archive outside of merchandise research.

Nobody really thinks or talks about this, so I try to emphasize it as much as possible to really embed it in sellers' minds. It's vital.

YOU SHOULDN'T JUST BE RESEARCHING THE SAME PRODUCTS YOU'RE TRYING TO SELL.

Enter my little mini-research process inside Pinterest that is extremely simple, yet profoundly impactful.

On the next page you'll find the terms you're going to search on Pinterest (replace the word "wildflower" with any trend here)...

PINTEREST RESEARCH MINI-PROCESS

🔍 **WILDFLOWER <u>AESTHETIC</u>**

🔍 **WILDFLOWER <u>ILLUSTRATION</u>**

🔍 **WILDFLOWER <u>STICKER</u>**

🔍 **WILDFLOWER <u>QUOTES</u>**

Every one of these search phrases has a specific brain priming purpose.

We're going to talk about each now to break it down even further.

 WILDFLOWER AESTHETIC

"Aesthetic": This word, in combination with any given trend, will give you a general sense of what the trend is all about visually. It will also help you understand the underlying emotional connection piece behind why the trend is so in demand.

The photos to the right are some examples of what comes up for this search.

They're extremely useful for understanding the trend as a whole or the "feeling" behind the trend.

Believe it or not, this is a super important thing to fully grasp before you can begin creating designs that sell like hot cakes.

You must tap into the feeling.

if God gives
such attention
to the wildflowers,
most of them
never even seen,
don't you think
he'll attend to you,
take pride in you,
do his best
for you?

Luke 12:28

"Illustration": Here we're getting into some of the GOOD stuff. This search phrase has got to be one of my favorites of all my brain priming hacks. Because it allows you to see a bunch of creative designs that may not already be on merchandise.

What you'll find here is just pure, unadulterated creative juice. Most of my best creatively prompted ideas came from brain priming with illustrations.

The idea is simply that you're observing the details and making lots of observations. A cute quote, an interesting color palette, the simplicity of an outline design, etc.

Again, we're <u>not</u> trying to copy anything that we're finding.

We're allowing our subconscious (AKA your 'mental archive') to soak up the details of what we're looking at like a sponge - *because your subconscious will remember things you consciously won't when you sit down to create designs.*

Q WILDFLOWER <u>STICKER</u>

"Stickers": Stickers can be as much of a goldmine of creative inspiration as illustrations - because many times they're also unique designs that haven't been used on other products yet.

As you can see from the examples on the left, there are SO many cute ideas here from the layout of the design, to color choices, to unique little quotes and so many more details!

You're feeding your mental archive so much creative juice just by observing these designs and thinking about their details.

Have I convinced you yet to think outside the t-shirt box?

Q WILDFLOWER <u>QUOTES</u>

"Quotes": Our last category is quotes. This one is a big one because most designs sell easier with a meaningful, funny, or thought provoking quote included in the design.

HOWEVER, using the same quotes everyone else is using, which is a super common newbie mistake, isn't going to be very appealing to shoppers.

Why? *Because they see those quotes everywhere all the time.* They're boring and lacking emotional connection (*and strong emotional connection is what creates purchases, by the way*).

Some examples of these types of quotes are as follows (many of these are also trademarked, meaning off limits for commercial use):

- Be kind
- Live, laugh, love
- Mental health matters
- Be the good

There are SO many creative quotes or ways to creatively put a 'spin' on overly used quotes. Nobody should be regurgitating quotes like the ones above if they're really serious about making sales.

INSTAGRAM

Instagram is an absolute beast when it comes to feeding your mental archive what it needs to grow and expand at a rapid rate.

I LOVE me some Instagram brain priming.

But most sellers I work with are very confused as to how to make it work for them in terms of research.

So first things first:

CREATE A DESIGNATED INSTAGRAM ACCOUNT SPECIFICALLY FOR BRAIN PRIMING (RIGHT NOW!)

That's right. We're not researching on our personal or business accounts - *we're creating a brand new account that is exclusive to only researching activities.*

It is not an account you'll share with anyone. You can even immediately put it on private, but you don't have to because you won't actually be sharing or posting anything on this account.

The purpose of this account is to follow specific other accounts that post useful, research-worthy content. This way, you can wake up and check your designated IG account like the morning paper and scroll through a feed filled specifically with juicy brain priming visuals.

"OK, I CAN DO THAT, BUT WHAT ACCOUNTS SHOULD I FOLLOW?"

This is a common first question and an easy one to answer...

Do a little digging and go down rabbit holes. When you find one account that looks interesting, look into the similar accounts IG suggests after you hit follow.

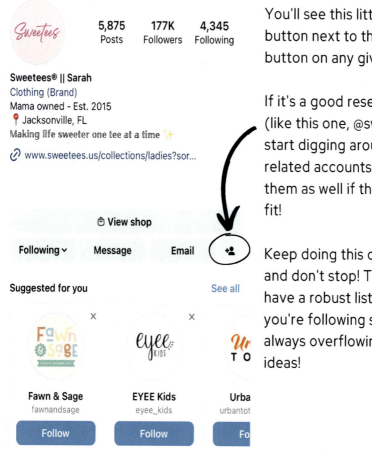

You'll see this little symbol button next to the follow button on any given account.

If it's a good research account (like this one, @sweetees_), start digging around at the related accounts and follow them as well if they're a good fit!

Keep doing this over and over and don't stop! The goal is to have a robust list of accounts you're following so your feed is always overflowing with good ideas!

I also wouldn't be doing my due diligence if I didn't mention that my monthly trend-spotting membership, Wolf School (**www.beawolfbiz.com/wolfschool**), has an exclusive Instagram account that only students in the membership can follow.

This account, as it stands right now, is following over 600 accounts that I myself found and followed (after I deemed them worthy, of course).

This means that members, on their own designated trend-spotting IG accounts can click into that following list and follow those accounts as well!

This is a *very quick way* to get your designated account ready to rock n' roll. And just one of the many perks of Wolf School.

But I'm not going to leave you totally hanging here - no way. I've got a few accounts I'm happy to suggest to get you started:

- **@ashlee.illustrates** : Pretty and colorful design & quote inspo

- **@thepinetorch** : A powerhouse mystical design shop (that also kills it on Etsy!)

- **@wickedclothes** : Super creative goth inspired designs & quotes

- **@allyblaireco** : More unique designs & quotes

As you're developing your designated account remember it's not all about clothes. You're likely to find the most creative ideas in accounts other than clothing brands! So be open to it all and don't limit yourself around where inspiration could be hiding.

One final word on Instagram researching: I don't tend to use it for specific researching, although you can with the search function.

I like to use my designated account to get lots of general ideas on the daily - then take those ideas to Etsy and Pinterest to flesh them out even further if I want to.

I want to remind you one last time that there are no specific steps to this process...

THE ONLY WAY YOU CAN REALLY GET BRAIN PRIMING WRONG IS IF YOU'RE NOT DOING IT.

So don't let it frustrate or overwhelm you. Again, this process should feel *fun and free flowing*. Let yourself wander around and be led in different directions, even if you had a specific intended direction when you started. It's fine to veer off!

It's also OK, and preferable even, to let this process be "messy".

As long as you're actually doing it and saving what you find interesting so you can refer to it later if need be - you're on the right track!

I recommend at LEAST an hour a day of brain priming, but more if possible. Do it while you watch a movie, stand in line at the grocery store, sit at the park - wherever!

The less stuffy and serious you can make your perception of it, the better. Because, again, ***it's supposed to be fun.***

04

PART 2

My secret

DESIGN HACK TO CREATE MEGA BEST SELLERS

Once you've done the research and allowed yourself to absorb the types of designs your market is after when they search "wildflower shirt" (or any other type of product you may be hot on the trail of), now it's time for some action.

As I've previously stated, when you're researching, you're not doing it with an intent to copy anyone. We've already established that doing what everyone else is doing is <u>absolutely not what we're after here.</u>

We want to stand out from the competition and fit into what's high demand.

It's a balance.

The purpose of researching is to observe, generally speaking, what consumers are seeking and currently loving.

Then take these concepts and develop them into something unique.

Something irresistible that everyone is going to pounce on.

But *how*? Here's the trick...

TREND COMBINING

Trend combining is *a simple, yet extremely effective design strategy that has produced best seller after best seller in my shop.*

Let me break it down for you using my favorite example from quite a number of years back.

It's my favorite historical example because it was the first time I tried this little trick and the first time I experienced unbelievable results from it!

Although I was doing well after a year of opening my shop, I wanted to continue to scale. I started thinking about more ways I could differentiate and increase demand in my new listings.

I naturally began to gravitate toward combining popular trends I was already featuring in my shop as a way to stand out.

To be honest, I didn't even realize this tactic was one of the main elements contributing to the big results I was seeing until a few years ago. I wasn't even really aware I was doing it at the time!

But back to my example. At the time, I was selling very popular mermaid tops that looked like this...

And equally popular galaxy shorts that looked like this...

One day an idea dawned on me while I was thinking about the growing number of mermaid product competitors and how I could separate myself.

Why not create a galaxy + mermaid design?

And thus, a **mega best seller was born** out of a very timely fusion of trends!

I've replicated this trick over and over again and it almost always works like a charm. It excites people when they spot something so unique that oozes trendiness.

Everybody wants something that no one else has, and combining trends gives you, as a seller, the power to provide that to people.

Talk about a competitive edge!

Also, it's very important to keep in mind that trends can reach beyond just the elements that are incorporated in a design.

Trends can be colors, patterns, design placement, shirt styles, etc.!

When you're building a print on demand empire, you've got to be aware of *everything* that's trending.

But more on this later...

Let's apply this trend combo concept to our "wildflower shirt" example and see what we can come up with.

We've done the research and now have a sense of what people are looking for when they're searching for a wildflower shirt.

We've been able to observe what's out there and the sellers that are doing the best with these items (they're on the first page of search results, remember?).

Let's say you've spent a good amount of time brain priming in general.

You should have some ideas of other trends that could make sense with wildflowers.

Once you've got those ideas, then you can start playing around with how to creatively fuse them together.

Let's look at some examples of wildflower design trend combos to help sharpen your eye for what this looks like!

**WILDFLOWERS +
MENTAL HEALTH**

**WILDFLOWERS +
FAITH BASED**

**WILDFLOWERS +
BOOKCORE**

**WILDFLOWERS +
FEMINIST**

As you can see, these trend combos are all quite subtle in the way that not many people would observe them and say, "I love how those two trends are combined in that design!".

No, a shopper would likely just say, "I LOVE that design!".

And that's exactly the response we're aiming for.

Trend combos just make a lot of sense. The things you're combining should feel like they merge effortlessly.

Don't make the mistake of cramming things together that don't make sense for the sake of creating a trend combo.

You'll get better at understanding how to seamlessly create these combinations as you build your mental archive and get a lot of practice!

The best part about combining trends is that you're filling a hole that doesn't yet exist, and thus establishing your item as a listing that will likely pique shoppers' curiosity.

It's easy to get stuck thinking things are already too saturated and that there is no more opportunity for designs that stand a chance.

When you're combining trends, however, that problem becomes obsolete. Again, the sky becomes the limit!

HOW EXACTLY TO TREND COMBINE

After researching it comes the time to take a seat in front of your laptop and whichever design editor you prefer (my favorites are all linked up in the resources section of this book), and begin experimenting.

When I'm creating designs and "trend fusing" I don't put pressure on myself to create something majestic right out of the gate.

That's a surefire way to create something subpar because every step of the way feels intensely full of pressure and frustrating.

Just allow the process to unfold as it should. Step away and come back – multiple times if necessary.

The creative process requires space.

Many times it will take me 5-10 reworks of the same design to land on something that feels like it finally clicks.

And, oh, what a gratifying feeling that is!

The more you do this process, the better you'll be at it.

The more you research and familiarize yourself with current trends, the easier it will be for you to start making the right calls while creating your designs.

Your subconscious is a powerful thing and investing enough time into doing the correct research will affect those sub-levels of your mind in amazing ways.

This eventually provides you with the type of intuition necessary to help guide you toward the decisions that are going to blow up your business.

Yup, we're talkin' mental archive again, ladies and gentlemen!

All roads seem to always lead back to that goldmine you're cultivating between your ears.

So let's quickly recap...

• **Step 1:** Do the brain priming. Just do it! Day in and day out commit to growing your mental archive so you can create best seller designs with ease (thanks to the info stored in your subconscious).

• **Step 2:** Start with a niche you've identified as having a good amount of demand, then explore what other niches may blend well with it.

• **Step 3:** Sit down and get to designing! Allow space for the creative process and continue fusing the trends you chose to combine until you've settled on a design that you feel your target market is going to really resonate with and respond to.

• **Step 4:** Publish that product to your store and bask in your own glory as you relish this major accomplishment and look forward to the sales rolling in!

Now that we've thoroughly discussed my research and design tactics, we're going to dive a bit deeper into the many different aspects of trend.

05 *The many facets*
OF TREND & HOW TO
TAKE ADVANTAGE OF THEM

I mentioned briefly in the last chapter that trends go beyond how we typically think of them when we're approaching new item creation in our shops.

It's easy to think something like, "Ok, I'm seeing a lot of girl power quote shirts lately... I should also create a shirt with a girl power quote."

But this kind of strategy (or lack thereof) limits a trend to just the actual design, or in this example case, a quote.

Trends reach far beyond designs and with print on demand, there's enough options to be able to play with these different aspects when creating new items.

You can experiment with design, of course, but also with item color, design placement, and type of item.

That gives you a lot to work with to create something great that's in high demand!

So let's talk about these different aspects of trend available with print on demand...

1.) Item color

We'll start with item color as our first non-design related trend to discuss because it's the most obvious.

We all know every year, color palettes change and trending colors go in and out rather quickly.

In addition to being observant about what people around me and on social media are wearing, I love the website **www.whowhatwear.com.** They give really great (and often really accurate), color trend forecasts!

Side note: When you find websites like this, always bookmark them for future reference because they can be a major resource for your business.

When it comes to color, we have a ton of options with print on demand.

In addition to solid color options, AOP (all over print) apparel is on the rise. It is usually a bit more expensive, but allows sellers the ability to create their own colors, patterns, designs or whatever else and place it all the way across the garment (or sometimes even shoes/boots and other products too!).

Popular colors on Etsy include the basics, of course, like black and white, but also dusty neutrals, many variations of pinks and blue, and we can't forget tie-dye!

2.) Design placement

The placement of text graphics or designs is something that many, I'd venture to say the majority, of sellers overlook or don't consider at all.

Which is wild to me because there is **so much power behind placement!**

Can you guess the two trendiest design placements in these photos?

First we've got the small design, front/center/top of the garment placement. This is really popular on hoodies, but applying it to t-shirts or crewnecks works too!

You can use just words for this type of design placement, or include elements as well.

The second is back placement. Another ultra-popular one for hoodies, but also applicable to t-shirts and sweatshirts.

There really are zero limits for these type of designs, but most of them do take up the majority of space on the back.

I will say many sellers think they *must* do a front print as well along with the back print. This is false! Many shops, even large retailers, do well selling blank fronts with a back print. Which helps with profit margins greatly!

Both of these placements are just an example of what to keep an eye out for when you're trend spotting.

A few years back placement along the bottom side of t-shirts with very large writing was hot.

More recently has been sleeve designs as well!

These are all solid trends that can really help get your potential customers excited about your product.

Deliberate trendy design placement is a really easy way to do a trend combo and stand out from the crowd in a new way.

You could spend an afternoon researching some design trends and then testing them out with different sizing/placements and have some potential best sellers in the works that quickly!

Just remember, the goal is to combine trends and create the best, most exciting print on demand garments on the search page – so you've got to make sure both trends you're combining are up to par!

Just getting the placement right on a so-so, or overused design isn't going to get you the big results we're after.

Every decision you're making in terms of your product creation process should be well informed and intentional.

3.) Item style

There are many different item styles to choose from (t-shirts with pockets, oversized hoodies, tie dye crewnecks, etc.), and these forms can trend up or down just like anything else.

Sometimes item styles that are trending can make things quite easy for print on demand sellers, because if it's a hot enough trend you can add a very simple or small design and it will still *sell, sell, sell*.

This why it's always worth it to be <u>as observant as possible</u> when trend-spotting to gather enough information to predict the "up-and comers".

Take the Comfort Colors brand, for example - which is a brand of soft, oversized and sort of vintage looking clothing that shoppers are going crazy for on Etsy.

Many sellers are seeing an increase in sales just by incorporating this brand into their shop - even at a higher price point!

As a certain style of garment style grows in popularity, many times the print on demand providers will catch on quickly and begin to offer that item, if they don't already.

This was the case with Comfort Colors and tie dye in the last few years.

When an item style is trending, you want to be offering it in your online store quickly and get as many different quality designs on that style as you can!

Comfort colors tee in color "Ivory", transformed into an Etsy best seller with a trendy design & mockup!

All of these examples given are available with most print on demand suppliers, and I suspect as print on demand continues to expand and grow, *many more* options will become available as well.

You can spot what item styles are trending the same way you spot trending designs and placements.

You do this through research on Etsy, Pinterest and Instagram, observing the world around you, and choosing a few of your favorite retail sites/Etsy shops that are in your niche and watching them like a hawk!

If you're observant enough, you can catch onto trends long before they hit big box retailers, and therefore aren't widely available, and then supply the world with the items they're looking for but can't yet find very easily.

This is the whole premise I've built my online stores on, and as long as I continue to put in the work and fine tune my trend-spotting skills – it continues to work for me!

06 General vs specific
HOW TO CHOOSE A NICHE

Many sellers put off opening a print on demand shop because of the age old debate that can plague you into *complete and total inaction if you allow it to.*

That debate is whether to create a general store, which means carrying many different categories of products and designs, or a niche store, which focuses more on a specific category of products or design theme.

My advice for getting over this hurdle, to put it very simply and straight forward, is to **go general and niche down as you learn more about your market, if you so choose.**

People tend to think most things matter more than they actually do.

This topic is one of those things.

Of course, whichever you decide to go with matters, but <u>it's not something you have to nail from the start.</u>

Flexibility and the ability to adapt and change as you grow is pretty much a basic requirement as an online seller, especially if you have no prior experience in online retail sales.

What most sellers (or wannabe sellers) don't consider is the fact that *they can change, adapt, or grow out of their strategy or game plan at literally any time.*

As a matter of fact, not only can you, but you should!

Ideally, you could start with a general store and base your products off of diligent trend-spotting and try to have some common, general theme throughout – like adult tees and sweatshirts or baby onesies.

This is a good strategy because you are selling within a broad category, which allows enough room to test many different items and designs, but not too much room to where all focus is lost.

What you *don't* want is to end up with a shop that carries so many varying items and categories of items that things plateau at "ok," instead of excellent because you're so widespread and un-focused.

It is usually a good plan to eventually zero in on a very specific market/niche and learning that market so well that you are able to dominate it.

But if you're just starting, *you don't know what you don't know yet.*

So you have to **put in the time and experimentation to be educated enough in order to make the right decision on where you want your shop's focus to go!**

This is why I encourage sellers to start general and work their way into more focused categories.

Keep in mind, you can sell all types of print on demand items and still be a niche store.

A seriously trending category right now is the western niche. The general public is loving themselves some good cowgirl/boy inspired merchandise.

If you were to discover this opportunity among your research and feel it was a good fit for your shop, you could create western themed t-shirts, mugs, hoodies, stickers, and totes.

While some sellers may feel they would miss out if they niche down into a specific category, you can go narrow and still have pretty much endless opportunity.

Special note: I still don't recommend doing this at the start. You have to test, test and test some more to gather information about what people are actually going to want and buy from you first.

But what if you wanted to maintain a more general store for the lifetime of your shop?

There are many shops that have done this and been very successful, but there are definitely key things you have to keep in mind that make this a bit of a trickier scenario than creating a specific niche store.

First of all, there tends to be much higher competition among general shops. You're appealing to a much broader audience when you're not within a specific niche, so there will always be more competitors.

There is also less focus, as I mentioned earlier, so sellers have a tendency to arbitrarily trend chase (I call this squirrel brain behavior), instead of deliberately trend-spot within a specific category.

If you're really confused and don't know where to start or which option to choose, dig into the research and don't choose.

Begin quite broadly and narrow down your offering based on what you learn and discover.

As I've gone along in my e-commerce journey, I've stumbled on so many ideas simply by combing through magazines or blogs.

I'll have a sudden light bulb moment and have to create something right then and there to follow through with the spark to see if I can create anything meaningful out of it.

Those moments are powerful!

If you're seeing something frequently and a good amount of people are starting to gravitate toward it, it is likely a good idea to test a few different angles of that trend within your shop if it makes sense for you.

From there, you'll be able to gauge your market's reaction to the products and you can continue to create more and/or different versions of these products if the response is favorable.

Finding your niche often happens naturally through this process.

It's important to not try and force something when it's not getting great results and you can't seem to move the needle.

One fundamental truth I've discovered that proves itself over and over again the longer I am in this business is that **you must focus on what's working.**

Forget the rest.

Seriously! Test things and experiment until you feel you're onto something. Then build that thing out into new designs and/or products.

This is how niches sometimes come to develop in a natural way. You've followed a trail and came to a conclusion based on some solid experimentation.

In that case, you're not just jumping in feet first to a whole category of things that nobody cares about.

You've carefully crafted your product offering in a way that allows you to know for sure it's one that people care about and that you can continue to build out.

So here's a little bit of a game plan I've put together to spell out the process and help provide some clarity on how exactly you want to go about getting started with your online shop...

Step #1: *Always* begin with the research

You'll need to log some serious hours in the beginning of your print on demand journey studying various shops and online marketplaces to get your brain primed and used to trend-spotting (building that mental archive baby!).

Following the process outlined in chapter 4, you'll want to begin looking for the things that people are currently actively searching for online.

You'll also want to decide on a print on demand supplier and familiarize yourself with their product catalog so you're aware of what's available to you.

And a quick side note on that - you can work with more than one print on demand supplier if there are certain unique aspects to two of them that you'd like to take advantage of.

I know that many sellers think they have to just choose one provider, but there's nothing wrong with testing more than one, or even choosing a few if that's what serves you best.

But remember, try to keep things as simple as possible. I'd recommend starting to work with one or two P.O.D. partners in the beginning phases of your growth.

Now is also the time you want to decide on a marketplace.

Beginning in a marketplace as opposed to a stand alone website is typically a good idea because there is already a built in traffic stream that your own website cannot offer.

Etsy, Amazon Merch, and Zazzle are popular marketplaces for print on demand sellers.

Obviously I'm the biggest advocate of Etsy due to its built-in 200 million+ annual shopper stream and usability.

But, back to speaking of categories, as you go through this process, in your mind you can begin to narrow down the general category you feel makes the most sense for you.

Men's hoodies? Women's leggings? Toddler tees?

Or perhaps a product offering that includes all of these things but with a common design theme.

Step one is not the time to actually make decisions, however - it's when you should be exploring the plethora of options available to you!

Step #2: Put together a product offering with a broad focus

The term "broad focus" was chosen deliberately here.

Because you don't want to begin *too* general with zero direction. You want to build on a broad category but a focused offering.

As we discussed, this can be as simple as deciding to be in the women's clothing category.

You can begin by listing different women's designs in a few different promising niches (*because we're starting by testing and experimenting, remember?*).

Or perhaps you choose men's tees and decide to sell a variety of trendy male-focused designs you've discovered in your research.

Expect all of this to feel somewhat uncertain. But when you're first starting out, the uncertainty can be exciting when you have the right perspective.

You must realize that there will always be uncertainty where there is little experience. But as you move forward and take the necessary steps forward, you will discover all the right stuff in order to continue taking additional steps that make sense.

The less pressure that you apply at this time, the better. Let the answers unfold as naturally as possible.

Trust the process.

Step #3: Jump in!

The third step is to create your designs, choose your products, and publish them out to the world! This is where you really start to learn what your market is all about.

You'll be able to begin analyzing which listings get attention and which are rising to the top the fastest.

This initial information is absolutely invaluable.

Think about it – these first stages are likely the most formative timelines that will determine your more permanent future direction!

That's exciting!

Say you begin with men and women's tees. You may try many different designs and find a few of your best sellers are family oriented designs like "momma bear" or "dog dad," which have been very high demand for many years.

You could then take this information and start making some decisions.

You could focus your research to dig a little deeper into these types of designs and build out this category to include even more variations of these designs in your shop.

Then you continue to test, test, and test some more. You move through this process and keep moving forward as long as what you're doing is continuing to work.

This is how you arrive at a niche.

Slowly but surely you research, experiment and collect data from your customers – **paying less attention to what's not working and building on the success of what *is* working.**

If you decide to remain offering men and women's tees, you could also build out some "sub-niches" within your shop.

The same idea applies here, where you're testing and building out what's working, but in multiple categories within the same shop.

The downside of this is that the shop is much more general without a single clear target market, so it can be more difficult to build a loyal following (which is a definite pro of being a niche shop) and possibly more difficult to market.

As we covered earlier, the decision on the type of direction you take your shop is entirely up to you and it really shouldn't be made immediately or before you even begin.

You should always be led by what the market is revealing to you through your deliberate research and experimentation.

In summary, should you go with a general store or a niche store?

Start general and go niche if the data you gather from your market (their clicks, favorites, and purchases) points you in that direction.

Can I say it just one more time?
Trust the process.

BONUS #1:
RESOURCE LIST

This is a book about trends (or better put, *demand*) and how to become an expert at spotting and then leveraging demand to become a print on demand mega seller.

However, **I'm going to give you ALL my print on demand resources** – those that have to do with trend and those that don't, in order to help you more easily and confidently build your online presence.

If you're a newbie with little to no experience, you should be paying special attention, because resources can fill in the gaps as you learn the ropes and shortcut you to success much more effectively!

PRINT ON DEMAND PROVIDERS

Printful – www.printful.com

Printful is among the most popular choices for print on demand providers and I've worked with them extensively. I've found their prices to be quite a bit higher than others and their turnaround times can be a bit slower (depending on different factors).

However, they are one of the biggest, most trusted print on demand companies so as a starting point, you can't really go wrong.

Printify – www.printify.com

Printify is my P.O.D. provider choice that I've used for several years now. They have multiple different suppliers under the Printify umbrella, so you have options.

Each supplier will differ in their location, reviews, color choices, shipping price, turnaround times, etc.

It's up to you to decide what's most important for you and your shop and choose accordingly.

I like Printify because their suppliers prices are generally pretty cheap and their turnaround time is fast. I also like that they provide a premium account option where you can pay $29 dollars a month to get 20% off all products used for your orders.

If you're selling a good amount of products, this 20% off discount can go a long way!

If you're interested in starting with Printify, shoot me an email at support@beawolfbiz.com and I'll send over my affiliate link to register with!

Here are some other popular print on demand suppliers I haven't worked with directly but may be worth considering...

SPOD – www.spod.com

TeeLaunch – www.teelaunch.com

Zazzle – www.zazzle.com

Redbubble – www.redbubble.com

TeeSpring – www.teespring.com

There are new print on demand providers popping up all the time, so I'd suggest exploring all of them and deciding what may work best for you!

Remember, *you can always switch if something isn't working well for you and you can use multiple providers if needed as well.*

POPULAR ONLINE MARKETPLACES

As we discussed earlier, it's the smartest route to begin your print on demand journey on an online marketplace (like Etsy) because there is a built in traffic stream of shoppers who can find your items in search within that marketplace.

Selling from your own website can take a large amount of resources, know-how and ads budget to really get things flowing. Therefore, a marketplace can be extremely useful in the beginning.

Not every print on demand company is going to integrate with every marketplace. There are some that are definitely more limited. So make sure before choosing a provider that you know where you want to sell and can confirm that P.O.D. company integrates with that marketplace.

Here are some popular marketplace favorites...

Etsy – www.etsy.com

Ebay – www.ebay.com

Amazon Merch – www.merch.amazon.com

StoreEnvy – www.storenvy.com

DESIGN EDITORS

When you're a print on demand shop owner you've got to stay on top of trend and, like it or not, you've got to be able to create designs people want.

I am in no way a graphic designer but I've carefully chosen the best possible design resources in order to create simple, yet powerful, designs *that sell.*

When you've got the right resources, you don't necessarily have to be over-the-top talented (this goes for just about anything!).

Design is no exception.

Photoshop Elements

This is the editing software I use most frequently. It's a bit more advanced but allows me to do everything I need.

It's kind of like the basic, dummy version of Photoshop, but still with lots of functions and capabilities.

I love it because it's only around $60-80 and you can install directly onto your computer after purchase. Best Buy and Amazon are two retailers that sell PS Elements online for a good price.

Canva – www.canva.com

Canva is a resource that everybody who's anybody in the print on demand space knows about.

There is a free and a paid version and it is super user friendly.

This is most likely the best place to start if you're new to designing and a bit intimidated by the process.

Canva also supplies you with many different designs, fonts, templates and much more.

Most of these can be used legally with a pro account (with is about $10 bucks per month) because they come with a commercial license (meaning you can't get in any legal trouble incorporating these elements into your designs).

The free version is limited in what can be used, but the subscription is affordable and well worth it if you're using it as your main design creator/editor.

The pro version also comes with a super convenient 30-day trial so you can get give it a test run before committing to payment!

Picmonkey – www.picmonkey.com

Picmonkey is pretty similar to Canva, maybe with a few more photo editing capabilities. It also offers a free and pro version (with a 30-day free trial).

Which design editor you choose depends heavily on the types of designs you're creating and the functionalities that are most important to you.

If you don't know which to choose in the beginning, I'd recommend signing up for the free trials and testing them out with a few designs.

Choose whichever serves your needs best!

GRAPHICS & COMMERCIAL USE CLIPART

It's not required that you know how to create your own graphics or works of art to display on your items.

Most of the time trending designs are a simple combo of a few elements and/or fonts.

I've listed here a few of my favorite places to find commercial use graphics and clipart to incorporate into designs of all sorts.

As I mentioned previously, Canva is a useful editor because it supplies you with different commercial use design elements too!

But as a big, booming business owner you're likely going to need some more options.

Here are a few to get you started...

Creative Market – www.creativemarket.com

This is my most favorite resource for design elements of all types! It's an extremely popular platform for many different types of artists to sell their work.

Most of what you find on Creative Market can be bought with a commercial license for just a few extra bucks so it's safe to use it in your designs.

You can purchase fonts on Creative Market as well!

Most design elements come in bundles too, so you get the most bang for your buck.

Etsy – www.etsy.com

Yes! You read that right! Etsy is a great source of commercial use graphics and clipart (take this shop for example: **www.huckleberryhearts.etsy.com**)!

Start by searching "commercial use graphics" and look at all the results that come up.

There are tons of shops brimming with all kinds of design elements you can purchase and then incorporate into your own designs!

Vexels – www.vexels.com

Vexels can be highly useful for more advanced sellers who are looking to add even more options to their design arsenal. They even offer custom designs made just for you with their annual plans.

PHOTOS & EDITING

The last thing you want as a shop owner is to have spotted exactly the right trends, created perfect timely, winning designs, and then list your products with subpar listing photos.

Oh, *the horror!*

Photos of your products can absolutely make or break your shop and getting the right ones in place should be a <u>top priority.</u>

Ordering tons of samples of your products and constantly orchestrating photo shoots, however, is costly, time consuming and slows the process of getting items published way down.

I'm going to share with you my favorite solution to this problem...

DIGITAL MOCKUPS!

And here are just a few of my favorite resources to get them from...

PlaceIt – www.placeit.net

PlaceIt is a mockup website with thousands of mockup photos of all different types of products.

There are lifestyle or studio shots of clothing on models, or a selection of "flat lays," which are photos of just the products.

Placeit allows you to use their editor to place your designs onto whatever garment photo you choose and control the colors of the garment as well.

The best part is that the photos look fully realistic. The problem with most mockup photos is that they look very digital and fake.

Consumers are starting to be mistrustful of buying anything that looks like a mockup – in case what they actually receive looks different.

That's not something you have to worry about with Placeit.

Your design file appears as though it is integrated into the fabric and will give the effect that you put a whole shoot together just to get that shot!

Placeit is under $20 a month and an invaluable resource for print on demand sellers trying to save some time and cash.

You get unlimited access to as many of their photos as you need for that price!

PhotoToaster App

I already covered my go-to editing software, Photoshop Elements. I use this program for both creating designs and editing photos.

However, many times I want to be able to edit on the go.

This sweet little $2.99 app does just the trick.

It's got tons of features, but not too many that it's overwhelming or hard to get the hang of.

My favorite part of the app is that you can edit a photo and save all of the edits you did to a preset that can be applied to more photos with just a tap!

This way you can create multiple photos with consistent lighting and editing. It also lets you do all the basics like cropping, straightening, rotating and more.

Canva/Photoshop Elements

Here they come again to save the day!

I want to mention these two resources for photo editing as well because they're well worth it for all your design and photo editing needs.

Adobe Photo Shop Lightroom App

Lightroom is an Adobe editing software that is a bit more complex and more advanced, but packs a powerful punch when it comes to all of its features and functionalities.

My favorite part is the "presets" you can save which, like PhotoToaster that I mentioned above, are edits you make to one photo that you can save and apply directly to other photos.

With Lightroom you can purchase presets (I find them on Etsy) and download them to your Lightroom app!

This way you can pick a type of photo style you want, select a preset that fits and apply it to all your photos.

BONUS #2:
PINTEREST TRENDS TUTORIAL VIDEO

I put together a video for you on exactly how to use the Pinterest Trends tool to leverage important market data in your print on demand business...

I walk through an example of the process and how it can benefit your shop! Watch the video at the link below:

https://bit.ly/pinteresttrends

You can also follow me on YouTube for LOTS of additional free content at https://bit.ly/beawolfbizyt

CONCLUSION

The print on demand world is your oyster.

Now that you've got all the expert level knowledge on how to create winning designs by leveraging strategic research on current trend, there's one more step left for you to take...

Go out there and take action!

Many sellers spend so long torturing themselves with endless deliberation and end up going nowhere fast. Action is what moves you forward. Period.

I would highly encourage you to take what you've learned in this book *and simply begin.*

Once you have the tools and a few keys to get you started in the right direction, which hopefully this book has supplied you with, it's up to you to make things happen!

Whatever specific market you decide to focus on in your shop, let the guidelines in this book help keep you on track. Also, remember this is a step-by-step process that cannot be shortcut.

Do the work and you will be greatly rewarded with the personal and financial freedom a booming print on demand business can provide for you!

I'm so excited for you and I am here to support you!

One more important note before I leave you - since writing ***Blank to Bank***, I've realized how many print on demand sellers had no idea Instagram was such a brain priming *powerhouse* - and many have asked me to expand on my IG trend-spotting process further.

Because of this, I created a 7-series video course called ***Research Revolution.***

In it I focus primarily on my Instagram research process and show you how I find inspiration AND execute on it by turning it into designs inside Canva (you watch me do the entire process from A-Z in this program!).

If you'd like in on this sort of "Part 2" to Blank to Bank... **Join Research Revolution now** by going to:
www.beawolfbiz.com/researchrevolution

You can also join the **free Be A Wolf Biz Facebook mastermind group at** www.facebook.com/groups/beawolfbiz

And don't forget to follow me on Instagram for even more free and useful tips, tricks, live workshops and announcements at www.instagram.com/beawolfbiz

**THANK YOU SO MUCH FOR READING.
IT'S AN HONOR TO BE APART OF YOUR
E-COMMERCE JOURNEY! I HOPE TO
GET THE OPPORTUNITY TO INTERACT
WITH YOU SOON.**

Made in the USA
Las Vegas, NV
08 July 2024

92018910R00052